D0710318

COOL
PAPER ART

# KARAKURI

## PAPER MADE
## TO MOVE

MEGAN
BORGERT-SPANIOL

Checkerboard
Library

An Imprint of Abdo Publishing
abdobooks.com

# abdobooks.com

Published by Abdo Publishing, a division of ABDO, PO Box 398166, Minneapolis, Minnesota 55439. Copyright © 2020 by Abdo Consulting Group, Inc. International copyrights reserved in all countries. No part of this book may be reproduced in any form without written permission from the publisher. Checkerboard Library™ is a trademark and logo of Abdo Publishing.

Printed in the United States of America, North Mankato, Minnesota
052019
092019

THIS BOOK CONTAINS RECYCLED MATERIALS

Design: Christa Schneider, Mighty Media, Inc.
Production: Mighty Media, Inc.
Editor: Liz Salzmann
Cover Photographs: Mighty Media, Inc.
Interior Photographs: iStockphoto, p. 29; Mighty Media, Inc., pp. 1, 3, 4 (pattern), 5, 6 (middle), 7 (glue, scissors), 8–27 (all), 28 (pattern), 30, 31, 32; Shutterstock Images, pp. 4 (both), 6 (left, right), 7 (circle, square), 28 (both)

The following manufacturers/names appearing in this book are trademarks: Artist's Loft™, Elmer's®, Sharpie®

Library of Congress Control Number: 2018966248

**Publisher's Cataloging-in-Publication Data**
Names: Borgert-Spaniol, Megan, author.
Title: Karakuri: paper made to move / by Megan Borgert-Spaniol
Other title: Paper made to move
Description: Minneapolis, Minnesota : Abdo Publishing, 2020 | Series: Cool paper art | Includes online resources and index.
Identifiers: ISBN 9781532119446 (lib. bdg.) | ISBN 9781532173905 (ebook)
Subjects: LCSH: Paper art--Juvenile literature. | Origami--Juvenile literature. | Japanese paper folding-- Juvenile literature. | Paper folding (Handicraft)--Juvenile literature.
Classification: DDC 736.982--dc23

# CONTENTS

# KARAKURI

Karakuri puppets **originated** in Japan in the 1600s. Karakuri means "**mechanism**" or "trick." And that's just what these puppets were. They were mechanisms that tricked the eye.

The puppets were **automatons** that could move on their own. They did so with the help of weights, **pulleys**, springs, and other simple mechanisms. These mechanisms were often hidden from view. This gave people the **illusion** that the puppets had come to life.

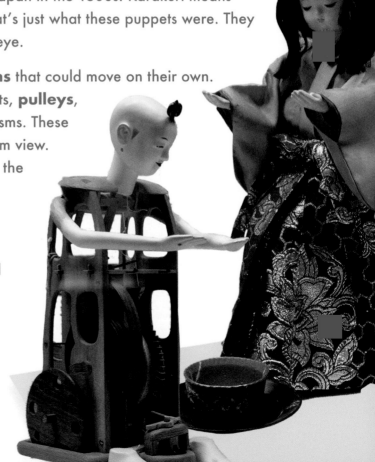

One of the most well-known examples of this craft was the tea-serving karakuri. The standing doll could move forward to deliver a cup of tea, then turn around and move back. These movements were **triggered** by the weight of a teacup as it was placed into or removed from the doll's hands. Other karakuri puppets could write, dance, and even shoot arrows!

Japanese karakuri puppets inspired the creation of mechanical paper art. Craftspeople in Japan and beyond have applied the simple, hidden **mechanisms** of karakuri to paper models. And you can do the same!

# MATERIALS

To make your own karakuri-inspired paper art, you'll need materials to make paper figures. You'll also need materials to create the **mechanisms**.

Here are some of the materials you'll need for the projects in this book:

## PAPER FIGURE MATERIALS

- card stock
- colored paper
- colored pencils, markers, or other drawing tools
- corrugated cardboard
- glue
- scissors

## MECHANISM MATERIALS

- corrugated cardboard
- craft knife
- foam tape
- glue
- matchbox
- nails
- pins
- plastic bottle
- straws
- tape
- wire
- wooden skewers

# THE BASICS

The projects in this book use several simple **mechanisms** to allow your paper art to move. These mechanisms include the slide, the **lever**, the **crank**, and the **cam**.

## SLIDE

A slide is a guiding surface along which something slides. The movement can be caused by pulling on a tab or forcing air through a straw.

## LEVER

A lever is a bar that **pivots** on a support called a **fulcrum**. When you push one end of the lever down, the other end rises. Anything attached to that end rises too.

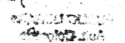

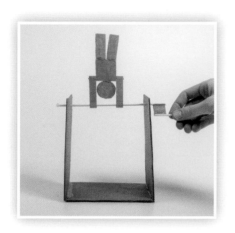

## CRANK

A **crank** is a bent handle attached to a shaft at a right angle. Turning the crank rotates the shaft. Anything attached to the shaft rotates too.

## CAM

A **cam** is a specially shaped part attached to a shaft. A rod rests on the edge of the cam. Turning the shaft turns the cam which pushes the rod up and down.

# PULL-TAB SCENE

- scissors
- card stock
- colored pencils, markers, or other drawing tools
- ruler
- marker
- craft knife
- glue stick
- foam tape

## 1

Cut a sheet of card stock in half crosswise.

## 2

Draw a scene on one of the halves. For example, you could draw a forest, a city skyline, or a body of water. Think of a moving object that would fit in your scene. It might be a bird, a car, or a fish.

**3**

Use a ruler and marker to draw a line where you want the object to move across your scene. Make sure the line does not reach the edges of the card stock.

**4**

Color over the line to make it about ¼ inch (0.6 cm) thick.

**5**

Have an adult help you use a craft knife to cut a slit around the line. This is the track for your object.

*Continued on the next page.*

## 6

Turn the scene facedown. Spread glue along the edges. Leave a 1-inch (2.5 cm) gap along the edge near the end of the slit. Press the glued side of the scene to the other half of the card stock.

## 7

Cut a strip of card stock that is ½ by 11 inches (1.3 by 28 cm). This will be the tab.

## 8

Slide the tab into the opening between the sheets of card stock. Push it in until the other end reaches the end of the track.

## 9

Use paper, markers, and other craft materials to create the object for your scene.

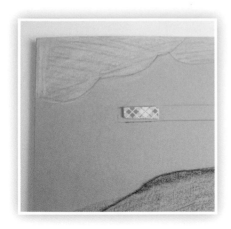

## 10

Cut a small piece of foam tape. Attach it to the tab at the end of the track.

## 11

Pull the backing off the top of the foam tape. Press the object to the foam tape.

## 12

Pull and push the tab to make your object move across the scene!

# HOPPING FROG

- 2 drinking straws, one thinner than the other
- tape
- paper
- scissors
- markers
- glue
- hammer
- nail
- plastic bottle with cap
- ruler
- hot glue
- straight pin

**1**
Pinch one end of the thin straw. Seal it with tape.

**2**
Use paper, markers, and other craft materials to create a frog.

**3**
Tape or glue the frog to the sealed end of the straw.

**4**

Have an adult help you use a hammer and nail to make a hole in the bottle cap. The hole should be just big enough for the thick straw to fit through it.

**5**

Cut a 1-inch (2.5 cm) piece off the thick straw. Slide the straw piece through the hole in the bottle cap. Seal any spaces around the straw with hot glue.

**6**

Slide the thin straw through the thick straw piece. The thin straw should move freely within the thick straw.

**7**

Push a straight pin through the thin straw below the bottle cap. Push the pin through at an angle so it will fit through the bottle's neck. The pin will keep the straw from coming out of the bottle.

**8**

Screw the cap onto the bottle with the pin end of the straw inside the bottle.

**9**

Squeeze the bottle to make the frog hop!

# PECKING BIRD

- ruler
- paper
- markers
- scissors
- 2 straight pins
- card stock
- empty matchbox
- glue
- wire

**1**

Use paper, markers, and other craft materials to create a bird. The bird should be about 3½ inches (9 cm) long.

**2**

Use a pin to poke a hole near the bottom of the bird.

## 3

Cut a small strip of card stock. Make it about 2 by ¼ inches (5 by 0.6 cm).

## 4

Fold the strip into thirds. This is the **fulcrum**.

## 5

Hold the ends of the fulcrum together. Use a pin to poke a hole through the ends.

## 6

Place the bird between the ends of the fulcrum. Line up the holes. Stick a pin through the holes. Leave the pin in place to hold the bird and fulcrum together. The bird should be able to **pivot** back and forth.

*Continued on the next page.*

**7**

Paint or decorate the outside of the matchbox. Glue the **fulcrum** to the top of the matchbox near one end.

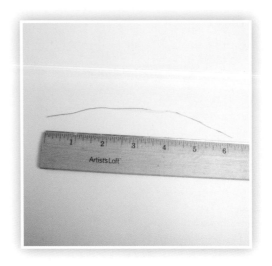

**8**

Cut a piece of wire that is about 6 inches (15 cm) long.

**9**

Open the matchbox nearly all the way. Use a pin to poke a hole in the end of the box.

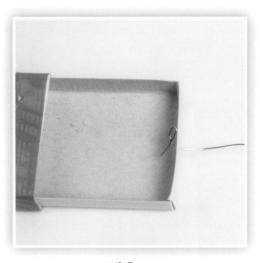

## 10

Push one end of the wire through the hole in the box. Make a loop in the end of the wire to keep it in place.

## 11

Use a pin to poke a hole in the bird's tail.

## 12

Thread the loose end of the wire through the tail hole. Make a loop in the end of the wire to keep it in place.

## 13

Open and close the matchbox to make your bird peck!

# SWINGING GYMNAST

- scissors or craft knife
- corrugated cardboard
- ruler
- pencil
- wooden skewer
- hot glue
- 2 thin nails about 1 inch (2.5 cm) long

**1**

Cut a piece of cardboard that is 5 by 3 inches (12.7 by 7.5 cm). This will be the base. Set it aside.

**2**

Cut two more pieces of cardboard. Make them each 6 by 3 inches (15 by 7.5 cm). These will be the walls.

**3**

Set one wall on the table. Draw a dot ½ inch (1.3 cm) from one end. Repeat with the other wall.

**4**

Use the wooden **skewer** to poke a hole through the dot on each wall.

**5**

Hot glue the ends of the walls that don't have holes to the ends of the base.

**6**

Cut your gymnast's head, body, and legs out of cardboard. Hot glue them together. The full height of the gymnast should be about 4 inches (10 cm).

**7**

Cut two cardboard rectangles for the gymnast's arms. Make them each 2 by ½ inches (5 by 1.3 cm).

**8**

Push a nail through the side of one arm near the top.

*Continued on the next page.*

**9**

Push the nail into the side of the body. The arm should be able to swing back and forth.

**10**

Repeat steps 8 and 9 to attach the other arm to the body.

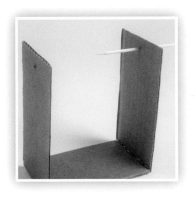

**11**

Push the **skewer** through the hole in one wall.

**12**

Push the skewer through both arms.

**13**

Push the skewer through the hole in the other wall. Carefully slide the gymnast to the center of the skewer.

## 14

Put a dot of hot glue on the end of the **skewer**. Let it dry. This will keep the skewer from slipping back through the hole.

## 15

Trim the other end of the skewer about 1 inch (2.5 cm) from the wall.

## 16

Cut a ½-inch (1.3 cm) square out of cardboard. Hot glue one edge of the square to the trimmed end of the skewer.

## 17

Cut a 1-inch (2.5 cm) piece off the leftover part of the skewer. Hot glue it to the opposite side of the cardboard square. Let the glue dry.

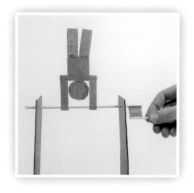

## 18

Turn the **crank** to make your gymnast swing!

# CRANK BOX AUTOMATON

- square cardboard box
- scissors
- 2 wooden skewers
- pencil
- drinking straw
- ruler
- hot glue
- blue chenille stems
- paper
- markers

**1**

Cut the top and bottom out of the cardboard box.

**2**

Use a **skewer** to poke holes through the center of both sides of the box.

## 3

Use a **skewer** to poke a hole in the center of the top of the box.

## 4

Use a pencil to make the hole big enough for the straw to fit through.

## 5

Push the straw into the hole. The end should reach just inside the box. Trim the straw about 3 inches (7.5 cm) above the box.

## 6

Cut two circles out of cardboard. Make them each 1½ inches (4 cm) across.

## 7

Use a skewer to poke a hole through the center of one circle. Poke a hole near the edge of the other circle.

## 8

Push a skewer through the hole in the right side of the box. Slide the cardboard circle with the off-center hole onto the end of the skewer. This cardboard circle is the **cam**.

*Continued on the next page.*

**9**

Push the **skewer** through the hole on the left side of the box. Make sure the skewer can spin within the holes.

**10**

Put a dot of hot glue on the end of the skewer. Let it dry. This will keep the skewer from slipping back through the hole.

**11**

Push the other skewer through the straw.

**12**

Slide the circle with the centered hole onto the end of the skewer. This circle should rest on top of the **cam**.

**13**

Adjust the cam so it is under the top circle but near the edge.

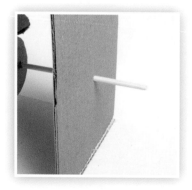

**14**

Trim the right end of the skewer about 1 inch (2.5 cm) from the side of the box.

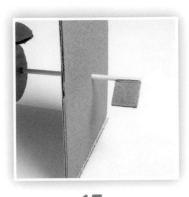

## 15

Cut a ½-inch (1.3 cm) square out of cardboard. Hot glue one edge of the square to the trimmed end of the **skewer**.

## 16

Cut a 1-inch (2.5 cm) piece off the leftover part of the skewer. Hot glue it to the opposite side of the cardboard square. Let the glue dry.

## 17

Trim the end of the other skewer about 1½ inches (4 cm) above the straw. Wrap blue chenille stems around the end of the skewer. This is the whale's spout.

## 18

Use paper and markers to create a whale. The whale should be about 2 inches (5 cm) tall.

## 19

Glue the whale to the straw so the spout is above the whale's head.

## 20

Turn the **crank** and watch the **cam** cause the whale's spout to move!

# CONCLUSION

Ancient karakuri puppets were impressive for both their mechanics and their artistry. Their simple **mechanisms** and carefully crafted models delighted viewers. The puppets seemed magical!

As you explore karakuri-inspired creations, experiment with different mechanisms. What different forms can a **crank** or **cam** take? In what other ways can you create a slide or **lever**? Try coming up with clever ways to conceal these mechanisms from viewers. Think of other paper figures you can make and explore new ways to make them move.

And like a true artist, keep your eyes and ears open for inspiration. Have an adult help you find online videos about the mechanisms of paper **automatons**. Try some of those methods. One day, you could be the one showing your paper art to the world!

# GLOSSARY

**automaton** – a machine that can move on its own without human control.

**cam** – a piece on a machine that slides or rotates, causing other parts to move.

**crank** – a device that transfers motion from one part of a machine to another.

**fulcrum** – the support around which a lever turns.

**illusion** – something that looks real but is not.

**lever** – a bar used to pull apart or move something.

**mechanism** – a system of parts working together.

**originate** – to start or begin.

**pivot** – to turn or twist.

**pulley** – a wheel over which a rope or cable may be pulled.

**skewer** – a long, pointed stick.

**trigger** – to cause something to happen immediately.

# ONLINE RESOURCES

**Booklinks**
**NONFICTION NETWORK**
FREE! ONLINE NONFICTION RESOURCES

To learn more about karakuri, please visit **abdobooklinks.com** or scan this QR code. These links are routinely monitored and updated to provide the most current information available.

# INDEX